# CRAFTS for kids

## Friendship Book

### Helen Skillicorn

**GROLIER**

90 Old Sherman Turnpike
Danbury, CT 06816

Published 2003 by Grolier
90 Old Sherman Turnpike
Danbury, CT 06816
A Division of Scholastic Library Publishing

© 2003 The Brown Reference Group plc.

**Set ISBN: 0-7172-5760-6**
**Volume ISBN: 0-7172-5775-4**

5278

For information address the publisher:
Grolier, 90 Old Sherman Turnpike, Danbury, CT 06816


Library of Congress Cataloging-in-Publication Data

Crafts for kids.
      p. cm.
   Includes indexes.
   Contents: [1] Backyard book—[2] Bedroom book—[3] Vacation book—[4] World book—[5] Winter
holiday book—[6] Back-to-school book—[7] Showtime book—[8] Bead book—[9] Valentine book—
[10] Dolls and bears book—[11] Ghostly book —[12] Games book—[13] Birthday book—[14] Fancy
dress book—[15] Friendship book—[16] Myths and tales book.
   ISBN 0-7172-5760-6 (set : alk. paper)
   1. Handicraft—Juvenile literature. 2. Cookery—Juvenile literature. 3. Games—Juvenile literature.
[1. Handicraft.] I. Grolier Incorporated.

TT160 .C747 2003
745.5—dc21

2002026405


**For The Brown Reference Group plc.**
**Craftperson:** Helen Skillicorn
**Project Editor:** Jane Scarsbrook
**Designer:** Joan Curtis
**Photography:** Martin Norris
**Design Manager:** Lynne Ross
**Managing Editor:** Bridget Giles
**Editorial Director:** Lindsey Lowe


Printed and bound in Singapore

# Contents

Introduction

Friendship Book is filled with ideas for special crafts to make for special friends. Make the Smile card on page 24 as a cheer-up gift or the Pirate portrait on page 22 for you and all your friends to have fun with—each can peer through the picture and get a photo taken as a grizzly pirate.

Each project includes a list of all the things you need. Before you go out and buy lots of new materials, have a look at home to see what you could use instead. For example, you can cut cardboard shapes out of old boxes. You may have candies, rice paper, and writing icing for the Fortune cookies in the cupboard, or you can buy them from a grocery store. You can buy clay and drawing inks from a craft shop and other items such as alphabet transfers from a department store.

## Getting started

Read the steps for the project first.

Gather together all the items you need.

Cover your work surface with newspaper.

Wear an apron, or change into old clothes.

### A message for adults

All the projects in Friendship Book have been designed for children to make, but occasionally they will need you to help. Some of the projects do require the use of sharp items, such as needles and scissors. Please read through the instructions before your child starts work.

## Making patterns

Follow these steps to make the patterns on pages 30 and 31. Using a pencil, trace the pattern onto tracing paper. To cut the pattern out of cardboard, turn the tracing over, and lay it onto the cardboard. Rub firmly over the pattern with a pencil. The shape will appear on the cardboard. Cut it out. To use a half pattern, trace the shape once, then flip over the tracing paper, and trace again to complete the whole shape. Or follow the instructions for the project.

# When you have finished

Wash paintbrushes, and put everything away.

Put pens, pencils, paints, and glue in an old box or ice-cream container.

Keep scissors and other sharp items in a safe place.

Stick needles and pins into a pincushion or a piece of scrap cloth.

# BE SAFE

Look out for the safety boxes. They will appear whenever you need to ask an adult for help.

Ask an adult to help you use sharp scissors.

# Linking lockets

This is a craft for you and your soul mate.
The two pendants fit together to make a
whole heart. They will remind you of your
best friend even when you are apart.

**YOU WILL NEED**

| | |
|---|---|
| air-drying clay | paintbrush |
| clay cutter | ribbon or thick |
| rolling pin | thread |
| paint | star sequins |
| varnish | glue |

**1** Roll out the clay to a
thickness of ¼in (0.5cm).
Cut out a heart shape, and cut the
heart in half with a zigzag line.

6

**2** Make a hole at the top of each half using a pencil. Let the clay dry and harden. Paint both pieces pink.

**3** When the pink paint is dry, paint dots and hearts in red and yellow onto the pendants. Go around each shape with a border of tiny dots in blue or yellow. We have glued on tiny star sequins, too.

**4** Paint a stripy border in blue, red, and yellow around each piece. Let the paint dry. Varnish the heart pieces. Let them dry.

**5** Thread ribbon or strong thread through the holes to make pendants. Give one half of the heart to a close friend.

# Hand in hand

When a classmate leaves school, make a wall hanging of linking hands as a leaving gift. Each person in the class decorates a hand patch in his or her own distinctive way.

**YOU WILL NEED**

| | |
|---|---|
| scraps of fabric | ruler |
| felt in different colors | pencil |
| | glitter glue |
| | sequins |
| wooden dowel | fabric paint |
| thin rope to hang up the hands | fabric flower |
| | glue |
| | scissors |
| cardboard | thin wire |
| hole punch | |

**1** Cut squares of cardboard 6in × 6in (15cm × 15cm). Make one for each of your friends to decorate. Make a hole in each corner using a hole punch.

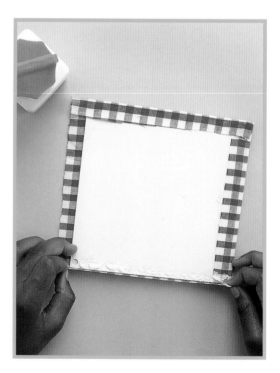

**2** To decorate your square, cover the cardboard with fabric, and glue down the edges on the back of the square.

8

**3** Draw around your hand onto felt, and cut out the shape.

**4** Glue the hand onto the fabric square. Paint on a design using fabric paint, or glue on a fabric flower. We have glued on sequins and stuck on stickers to decorate some of the hands. Have fun, and sign your name on the back of the square with a goodbye message for your friend.

**5** To make links to hold the squares together, wind wire around a piece of wooden dowel. Ask an adult to cut the wire spiral into circle sections.

Ask an adult to cut the wire links for you.

**6** Poke the wire links through the corners of the fabric squares to make up the hanging. Push a length of wooden dowel through the top row of wire links. You can hang up the hands by tying a length of thin rope to either end of the dowel.

# Bubble book

Make this beautiful bubble print
paper to cover a book
full of friendship memories.
Glue in notes and cards from
your friends and photos of you all.

## YOU WILL NEED

| | |
|---|---|
| washing-up bowl | drawing inks |
| | white paper |
| washing-up liquid | scrapbook |
| teaspoon | glue |
| | scissors |

**1** Add a slug of washing-up
liquid to a big bowl of water,
and swish it around with your
hand to make lots of bubbles.

**2** Trickle different colors of ink on top of the bubbles. Do this quickly, and get right to the next step!

**3** Lay a large sheet of white paper lightly on the bubbles. Take it off, and let it dry. You can print a few sheets from the same mixture.

**4** To cover a large scrapbook, you may need to glue together two or more pieces.

**5** Glue the paper to the outside of a scrapbook. Trim the edges. Glue a paper label to the front so you can write your name on the book.

# Fortune cookies

Write messages, dares, or fortunes for your friends, and put them in these edible packages. They're great fun to hand out after a meal.

## YOU WILL NEED

pencil
compass
rice paper
pinking shears
writing icing

strawberry
shoelaces
candies
paper and pen
hole punch

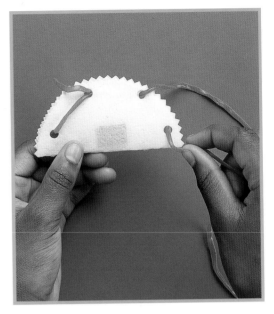

**1** Draw circles onto rice paper using a compass. Our circles have a diameter of 4in (10cm). Cut out the circles inside the lines using pinking shears or scissors.

**2** Fold a circle in half, and make four holes around the open edge using a hole punch. Write your message on a piece of paper, and slip it inside the cookie.

**3** Use a strawberry shoelace to lace the cookie closed. Tie together the ends of the shoelace.

**4** Stick on candies with icing to make faces. Decorate the candy faces with writing icing.

# Woven bracelet

Weaving a bracelet for a friend shows how much you care. To make this bracelet, weave ribbon through holes in a plastic frame. Take time designing the pattern before you begin.

## YOU WILL NEED

- large plastic drink bottle
- black marker pen
- scissors
- thin red ribbon
- thin blue ribbon
- thin yellow ribbon
- wide flowered ribbon
- beads
- felt-tip pens
- graph paper
- hole punch

**1** Cut a strip 2in (5cm) wide from a large drink bottle. Draw around the piece of plastic onto graph paper so you can design your bracelet.

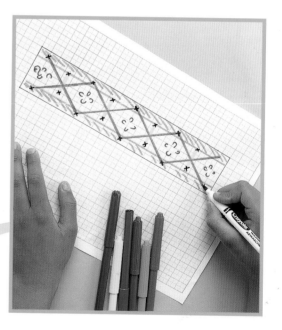

**2** Using colored felt-tip pens, draw a design onto the graph paper. Mark holes with black crosses, and plot which color ribbons you will thread through the holes. Copy our design on page 30, or make up your own.

14

**3** Lay the plastic strip over your design, and mark the crosses on the plastic, following the pattern. Punch holes where you have made crosses, using a hole punch.

**4** Begin by threading a thin blue ribbon along the top edge. Thread the ribbon in through the first hole and out through the next hole all the way along, then work back, filling in the gaps on each side. Now thread the red ribbon through, zigzagging across, and then zigzagging back to make crosses. Thread blue ribbon along the bottom edge.

**5** Thread thin yellow ribbon in stripes going down. Now pass a wide patterned ribbon under all the other ribbons around the middle of the bracelet. To finish, tie the ribbon ends together, and tie beads onto the ends of one or two of the dangling ribbon strands.

# Message decoder

Make a decoder for you and one for a friend. Turn the dial to set a code. Write a message using the letters you read off on the silver dial. Only your friend will be able to figure out the code!

## YOU WILL NEED

| | |
|---|---|
| shiny red cardboard | paper fastener |
| shiny silver cardboard | ruler |
| | scissors |
| alphabet transfers | sequin stickers and sequin waste to decorate |
| compass | |
| pencil | glue |
| felt-tip pen | masking tape |

**1** Draw a circle with a diameter of 4in (10cm) on shiny red cardboard. Draw a smaller circle on silver cardboard and an even smaller circle on shiny red cardboard. Cut them out.

**2** Lightly stick the silver circle on the big red circle in the center using masking tape. Rule a line through the center to divide the circles in half. Measure slightly less than ¹⁄₂in (1.2cm) along the edge of the circle from this line, and make a mark. Draw a line from this mark through the center of the circle. Repeat to divide the circle into 26 equal segments.

16

**3** Use transfers or a pen to mark a letter of the alphabet in each segment of both circles as shown.

**4** Decorate the small circle by gluing on sequin waste. Make a question mark with silver stickers.

**5** Stick silver sequin braid on the back of the big circle so it sticks out around the edge. Take off the masking tape and attach the circles together using a paper fastener.

# Tropical drink tray

Why not have a slumber party with a Hawaiian twist for your friends. Make a flowery tray to serve drinks. We have hollowed out melons to make little juice cups.

## YOU WILL NEED

round tray
green fake
    fur as big
    as the tray
pink, orange,
    and yellow
    crêpe paper
pink, orange,
    and yellow
    long pipe
    cleaners

gold glitter
florist's wire
florist's tape
pink, orange,
    and yellow
    acrylic paint
paintbrush
fabric glue
scissors
marker pen

**1** To make the flowers, roll up crêpe paper, and then cut a section 5in (12.5cm) long. Cut a section of orange and pink paper, too. Cut a point into one end of the crêpe sections as shown.

**2** Unroll the crêpe paper, and cut the strips into five-petal pieces. You will need three of each color. Brush orange paint onto the yellow petals and along the edges, and add dots all over the petals, too. Paint the pink petals with yellow paint and the orange petals with pink paint.

**3** To make the flower stamens, bend two pieces of pipe cleaner in half. Twist florist's wire around to keep them together. Choose pipe cleaners to match the color of the paint you used for each flower. Dip the ends of the stamens in glue and then glitter.

**4** Wrap the petals around the stamens and wire. Wind florist's tape around the bottom to keep them in place.

**5** Draw around a round tray onto green fake fur fabric. Cut around the circle, leaving 1in (2.5cm) around the edge. Make snips in this border, and fold in each tab, gluing it down to make a neat edge.

**6** Snip small holes around the edge of the fabric, and push the flowers through. Tape down the wire stems at the back. Place the grassy cover onto the tray, and pile on the midnight feast!

# Green grub frame

Keep photos of
your closest
friends next to one
another in this grub
frame. It will
look as if
the grub has
gobbled
them up!

## YOU WILL NEED

- four curtain rings
- green poster paint
- paintbrush
- green cardboard
- one pink and two yellow pipe cleaners
- two yellow pompoms
- pencil
- clear glue
- stiff white cardboard
- scissors
- black marker pen
- green fake fur

**1** Unscrew the brass eyes from the curtain rings. Draw around a ring onto green cardboard. Draw and cut out four green circles in this way.

**2** Glue the rings to the cardboard circles. Only glue half way around, so there is a gap to slip in a photograph.

**3** On a piece of white cardboard draw the grub's body and head. Draw around a curtain ring to get the shape right—the body is four circles in a row. Cut out the shape.

**4** Glue the rings onto the grub. Paint the rings and the background green. Leave white spaces for the eyes. Draw on a face, and glue on pipe cleaners with pompoms for antennas. Glue on a tuft of fake fur hair, too.

**5** Cut four pieces of yellow pipe cleaner, and bend them into V-shapes with feet. Put them over the grub between the rings, so that the photo frame stands up.

**6** Cut out pictures of your friends, and slip them into the ring frames.

# Pirate portrait

Have fun peering through the pirate portrait. Take photos of each other, and then try painting a different character's portrait.

## YOU WILL NEED

large cardboard rectangle (the side of a cardboard box is best)
paintbrush
poster paints
scissors

tracing paper
pencil
gold spray paint
ruler
cardboard for frame
double-sided tape

**1** Paint the cardboard white. This is a base coat to make the other colors show up well.

**2** Trace the pirate's face on page 31. It is a half pattern so flip the tracing over, match the center lines, and trace again. Go over the pencil lines on one side. Now transfer the tracing onto the white cardboard following the instructions on page 5. Trace the hook, and transfer that onto the picture underneath the face.

22

**3** Ask an adult to cut out the pirate's eye area and the mouth. She or he will find it easiest to use a craft knife.

Ask an adult to cut out the pirate's face using a craft knife.

**4** Draw on a collar to finish the portrait. Now paint the pirate. Start with blocks of color, and then add shading in a different color. For example, add blue shading over the black beard.

**5** Ask an adult to cut a frame for the portrait out of cardboard. Take the frame outside, and spray it gold. Stick it to the front of the portrait using double-sided tape.

# Smile card

If you fight with a friend, this sad/happy clown card will cheer them up. Write a message on the back to say why you miss them and want to make up.

PULL

## YOU WILL NEED

| | |
|---|---|
| white cardboard | poster paints |
| yellow cardboard (8½in x 11in 21.5cm x 28cm) | paintbrush |
| | glue |
| | black marker pen |
| felt-tip pens | shiny paper for the bow tie |
| scissors | stick-on sequins |
| tracing paper | |
| pencil | alphabet transfers |
| thin gift wrap ribbon | |

**1** Fold the yellow cardboard in half widthwise to find the center. Now unfold it, and fold the two edges into the center.

**2** Trace the happy clown face on page 30. It is a half pattern, so flip over the tracing, and trace again to make the whole face. Go over the pencil lines on one side, then transfer the tracing onto white cardboard following the instructions on page 5.

24

**5** Paint the smiley clown's lips red, and paint on pink cheeks and a stripy outfit. On the sad clown paint the mouth red, and paint green strips above the eyes. Let the paint dry. Go over the eyebrows and lips with a pen.

PULL

**3** Cut out the clown, and glue it to the middle of the yellow cardboard—his ears will stick out over the edges. Cut out the eyes and a slit for the mouth as shown on the pattern.

**4** Trace the sad clown pattern on page 30, and transfer it onto white cardboard. Cut out the shape and the mouth slit as shown on the pattern.

**6** Fold back the yellow card edges, and tape them at the back. Slip the sad clown inside so that the mouth tab pokes out. Mark "Pull" on the tab at the top with transfers. Decorate the hat with shiny paper and stickers, and fold shiny paper in a concertina to make a bow tie. Curl gift-wrap ribbon by running closed scissors along each strip. Glue it on to make frizzy hair.

# Sunshine badge

*Show the sunbeams in your life that you care! Make fun badges with different shapes and messages as surprises for your friends on special days.*

**YOU WILL NEED**

| | |
|---|---|
| yellow craft foam | brooch back |
| compass and pencil | thin scrap cardboard |
| gold glitter pen | scissors |
| glue | orange and gold paint |
| | paintbrush |

**1** Draw a circle onto yellow craft foam using a compass. Our circle has a diameter of 2½in (6cm). Draw two small flame shapes on scrap cardboard. Cut them out, and draw around them to give the sun a flaming edge.

26

**4** Decorate the center of the sun with gold glitter. You can write on a message with a gold glitter pen. We have written, "You are my..." (sunshine!)

**2** Draw a second circle onto craft foam, and cut it out. Cut out the flaming sun, too. Glue the circle on top of the sun.

**3** Paint orange and gold streaks onto the sun's flames.

**5** Glue a brooch back to the back of the badge.

# Claddagh box

The claddagh is an Irish symbol of love and friendship. It shows two hands clasping a heart. Decorate this tiny chest of drawers with purple velvet and a golden claddagh to make a dainty secrets box.

## YOU WILL NEED

| | |
|---|---|
| tracing paper | gold sequins |
| three | shaped like |
| medium-size | leaves |
| matchboxes | purple velvety |
| glue | fabric |
| purple poster | gold fabric |
| paint | pen |
| paintbrush | plastic jewels |
| purple craft | felt-tip pen |
| foam | tiny beads |

**1** Glue three matchboxes together, one on top of the other.

**2** Paint the individual drawers purple and the front edges of the chest purple, too.

**3** Cover the chest of drawers with purple velvety fabric. Glue a rectangle of fabric to one end of each drawer as well.

**4** Use three plastic jewels to make drawer handles. Glue each jewel onto craft foam, and cut out the foam around the jewel. Glue each handle to the front of a drawer. Glue a leaf sequin on either side.

**5** Copy the claddagh design on page 31 onto the side of the drawers. Go over the design using a gold fabric pen. Glue on beads at the crown tips and a yellow plastic jewel on the heart.

# Patterns

Here are the patterns you will need to make some of the projects. To find out how to make a pattern, follow the instructions in the "Making patterns" box on page 5. Some of the patterns are half patterns. There are instructions to help you use the half patterns in the steps for the project. The bracelet and claddagh designs are for you to copy. You don't need to copy them exactly; they are to help you with your own designs.

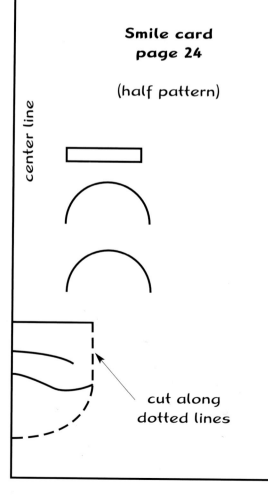

center line

**Smile card
page 24**

(half pattern)

cut along
dotted lines

center line

cut along
dotted lines

**Smile card
page 24**

(half pattern)

**Woven bracelet
page 14**

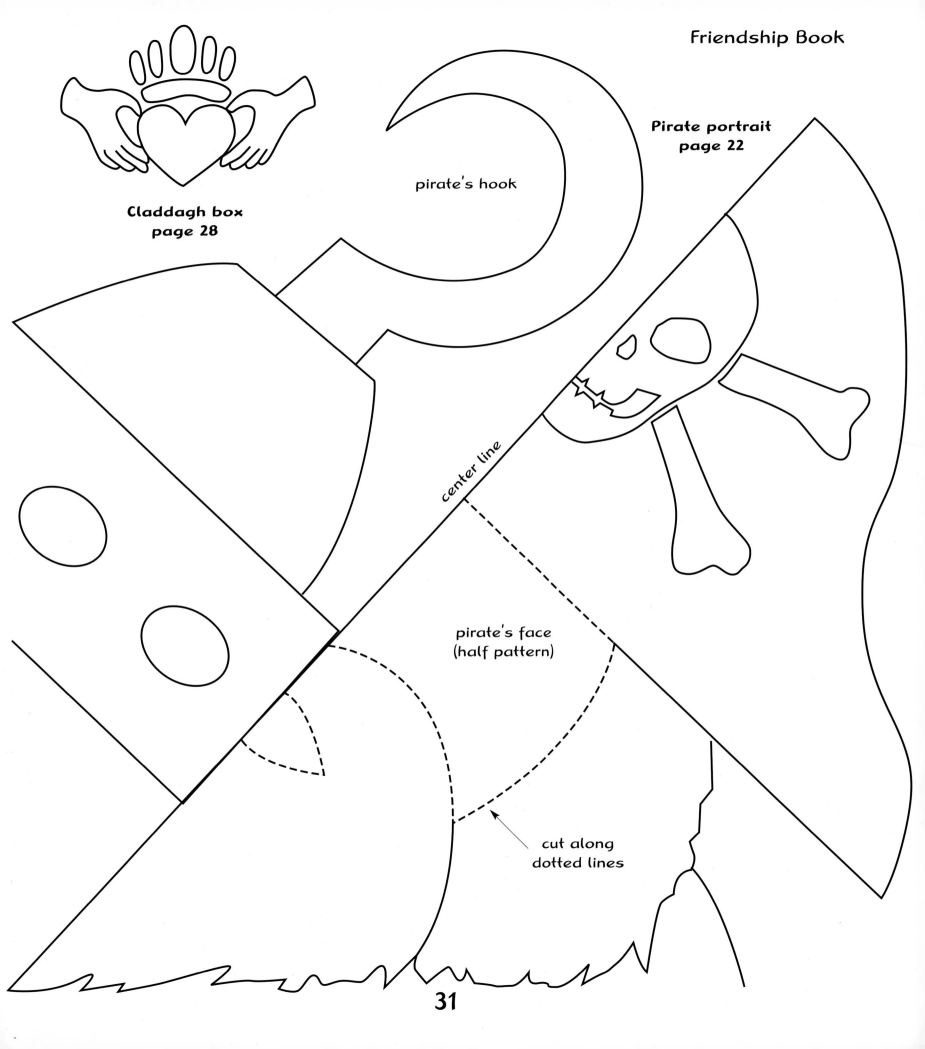

Claddagh box
page 28

pirate's hook

Pirate portrait
page 22

center line

pirate's face
(half pattern)

cut along
dotted lines

# Index